To

From

Look for places
to personalize this
book on pages 20,
21, 33, 41, 49, 51,
59, 69, and 79.

This book is dedicated to everyone who has ever influenced my life in any way.
You have been the instruments God has chosen to mold and shape me into who I am today.
I thank God for each of you, for apart from you my life would be empty and without meaning.

God bless you and keep you in His love!

My Mom & Mom-in-Love

My Siblings — all 6 of them!

My Husband, Michael

My Daughter, Michelle

My Son-in-Love, Gary

My Granddaughters, Alexis & Jessica

My Teachers & Mentors

My Friends & Foes

The Samaritans & Strangers along my way

My Father, His Son, Jesus, & the Holy Spirit

One of a Kind

by God's Design

written and illustrated by

Karla Dornacher

THOMAS NELSON
Since 1798

NASHVILLE DALLAS MEXICO CITY RIO DE JANEIRO BEIJING

Dear Friend,

Have you ever been in a group of people and felt like you stuck out like a sore thumb, not quite fitting in? Have you ever compared yourself to other women and not measured up? We all long to fit in—to be loved, accepted, and valued for who we are—but sometimes the problem is that we don't know who we really are. But I have good news: God knows and so can you!

Not so many years ago, I felt very out of place in the world. I was stuck in a mindset of comparing myself to others, especially one particular group of women, and I thought if only I was more like them, then I would be accepted and gain their friendship. I tried to fit in but to no avail. Then one day God spoke to my heart and clearly showed me that by trying to be like these women, I actually had set them up as idols and given them the place in my heart that only He deserves. I never would have understood that on my own, so I knew that insight had to be from God! He told me that He had not created me to be a Kathy or a Peggy or a Sandi—He created me to be me. He said if I would quit trying to be like other people and seek only to be the woman He uniquely designed me to be then He would give me the desires of my heart, even desires I didn't know I had. And He has been faithful.

You also are uniquely His—one of a kind by God's design! My prayer is that through the pages of this little book you will be inspired and encouraged to discover and become all that He has divinely designed you to be!

In Christ's love and for His glory,
Karla

For some people, looking back on their lives is like delighting
in a scrapbook filled with fond memories.
For others, looking back is painful.
But what a joy we have, my friend, to believe in a God
who is able to take all the days of our lives—
the good, the bad, and the ugly—
and turn them into works of art exquisitely beautiful.
Our God is able to take a life once broken and battered
and transform it into a vessel of great value—
a life filled with love overflowing.

We each have our own story—a unique God~written novel of our days
that was penned before we were even born—
an eternal scrapbook created and kept by our heavenly Father.

The psalmist wrote,

"Your eyes saw my substance, being yet unformed.
And in Your book they all were written,
The days fashioned for me, when as yet there were none of them."

Psalm 139:16 NKJV

God knew before you were even born what your days would look like.
He knew how your story would unfold.
Your days were fashioned. They didn't just happen by accident.
Each day has been divinely designed—handwritten by the ink
either of God's sovereign will or His permissive will—
in such a way as to bring about the greatest glory
to the Author of your story and the greatest blessing for you.

When you look back over the path of your life and realize
that no one else has ever walked where you've walked,
experienced what you've experienced,
or been influenced by the people you've known, you truly begin to see
that no one else on the face of this earth is quite like you.

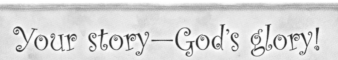

Your story—God's glory!

$\mathcal{A}$s I think about you, I wonder—where have you been all your life?
Do you still live in the house where you were born
or have you lost count of the places you've called home?
Has the path you've traveled been relatively smooth thus far
or has it been a rough and rocky road?

$\mathcal{W}$ithout question, where you've been influences who you are today.
The events of your life—celebrations or the lack of them,
as well as tragedies or the absence of them—
all contribute to how you view yourself
and how you connect with the world around you.
And the people along your path—parents, grandparents, siblings,
friends, teachers, children, even total strangers—
all have left their imprints, good or bad, on the fiber of your being.

God wants to use the circumstances of your life—past and present,
painful and pleasant—to draw you closer to Himself
and closer to becoming the woman He's designed you to be.

$\mathcal{A}$s you continue your journey through this book
and through your life,
may the path before you be brightened by God's Word
with a greater understanding of who He is,
who He says you are,
and the vision He has for the days still before you.

Your word is a lamp to my feet and a light to my path.

Psalm 119:105

LOVE passionately!
Be God's hands & heart to others.

LIVE abundantly!
Savor the moments of the ordinary.

LAUGH heartily!
Walk in the joy of the Lord and be glad.

GOING HOME

HEAVENLY GATE

LOVE · JOY · PEACE · PATIENCE · KINDNESS

MAP ~

Life is a JOURNEY

You have made known to me the PATH of LIFE; you will fill me with joy in your presence, with eternal pleasures at your right hand.

Psalm 16:11 NIV

I was in Atlanta, Georgia. I knew where I needed to go,
but I had no idea how I was going to get there.
Even though I had directions, they were terribly confusing,
and I was unsure if I would be going the right way.
And yet, even with my track record of getting lost
and a less-than-trustworthy roadmap, I was confident.

My JOY and PEACE OF MIND came from knowing I wasn't alone.

My daughter, Michelle, was with me. We were both going to the same place.
The blessing was that she had been there before and knew the way.
All I had to do was follow her.
I didn't need to look for signs, question if I was taking the right train,
or worry whether I was turning in the right direction.
My job was simply to keep my eyes on my daughter and stay close enough
not to become distracted or separated by other people or things.

My confidence was in Michelle and in her ability to lead me where I needed to go.
The success of my journey was not determined by my own ability
to follow directions but by my commitment to follow in the footsteps
of the person who knew the way.

What a great picture God painted for me that day!
He painted it for me to share with you, too. Can you see it?

We want Him to give us daily directions to follow.
He simply wants us to follow Him.

He wants us to be CONFIDENT and know that we're NEVER ALONE wherever we go

TRUST in THE LORD with all your heart, lean not on your own understanding.

ACKNOWLEDGE HIM in ALL YOU DO

and He will direct your paths.

Proverbs 3:5, 6 NKJV

Show me Your ways,
O Lord,
teach me Your paths;
lead me in Your truth
and teach me

Psalm 25:4, 5 NKJV

Skim back through the past chapters of your life story, and list a few of the people and events that have most influenced who you are today.

What are some of the godly attributes God was able to develop in your life through these experiences and people?

In the beginning, God created!
It is His nature to create, and I love that about Him!
Our God is the Author of all creativity and the Father of all creation.
All things were created by Him and for Him . . . including you.

God began to paint your portrait before time even began.
He used the finest brushes and the most beautiful pigments.
And, oh my, He was creative . . . just look at you!
A one of a kind masterpiece~fashioned in God's image and for His glory!

With a steady and tender hand, He began with your heart.
God carefully outlined your life with the amazing hues of eternal love,
and He colored your days with a splendid rainbow of potential and promise.

He continues to add touches of radiant color to the canvas of your life
moment by moment and day by day
as you aspire to become all He has designed you to be.
As you allow Him to refine your character and define your nature,
you continually look more and more like His beloved Son, Jesus.

You are God's handiwork, created on purpose and for a purpose~
to influence the world around you for good.
You do **MAKE A DIFFERENCE** in your world!

God has big dreams for you. Do you believe it? He does!
And He wants you to believe big for what He desires to do in your life.

He designed us to be visionaries and then told us in the Bible that
He is able to do more than we could possibly imagine or envision.
God knows that when we dream big and put our faith in the
enormity of who He is, He gets all the glory and we get blessed.

God has given us imaginations to see beyond what is,
and with this incredible ability we have the means
to unlock the potential, power, and possibility
that He has pre-designed into our lives.

Think about it . . . how do you see yourself?
Is your self~image based on hurtful words from your past
or are you using your imagination to see yourself through
God's eyes and the truth of who He says you are?

Each of us has been given a measure of creativity
that plays a part in painting our days and our destinies.
The brush God has handed us is called "choice,"
and as believers in Christ we are called to paint
from the palette of God's truth
with the colors of love, hope, faith, and obedience,
which are sure to brighten the darkest of days.

So dream big, trust the Dreamgiver
and always remember . . . you cannot out-imagine God!

Now faith is being sure of what we hope for and certain of what we do not see.

Hebrews 11:1 NIV

LOVE JOY PEACE

Dream Big

God is able to do exceedingly, abundantly above all that we can ask or imagine, according to His power at work within us.

from Ephesians 3:20

You are not only God's creation—a portrait of great beauty—
but He also chose you and adopted you as His own.
He takes great pleasure in having you as His child—
not because of what you do but because of who you are . . . His beloved daughter.

Imagine that you are a painting on the wall. Do you see yourself
as a watercolor, soft and flowing, or are you a bit more whimsical and fun?
Maybe you are a serious, realistic style, or possibly you're a collage—
a style more eclectic or eccentric in nature.

As God's child, your portrait hangs in heaven's hall of fame,
a priceless work of art . . . and God smiles and delights in you.
Did you know He smiles at you? He does!
God created the smile, so why wouldn't He smile at you, His beloved daughter?
In fact, God carries your photo in His wallet wherever He goes.
Every chance He gets, He opens it to your picture
and, as proud as any Father could be, He says,

"This is my *precious little girl*. Can you see the resemblance?"

And isn't it great that not all our portraits look alike? How boring that would be!
What a joy to know that each of us, in our own unique ways, can bring
GLORY TO THE LORD and **A SMILE TO HIS FACE!**

Who has smiled at you lately? How did you feel?
Take a few moments to sit quietly and imagine Jesus smiling at you.
How does knowing that God is smiling at you make you feel?

_____

_____

_____

_____

_____

_____

_____

_____

_____

_____

_____

_____

_____

_____

_____

_____

_____

_____

Delight yourself
in the LORD,
and He will give you
the desires of
your heart.

Psalm 37:4 NASB

Delight, verb 2. to keenly enjoy,
take great pleasure in, rejoice in,
find deep contentment in,
be extremely satisfied with,
find refreshment in.

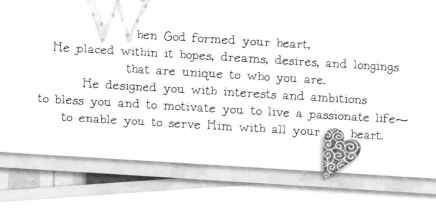

When God formed your heart,
He placed within it hopes, dreams, desires, and longings
that are unique to who you are.
He designed you with interests and ambitions
to bless you and to motivate you to live a passionate life—
to enable you to serve Him with all your heart.

Are you passionate about encouraging and comforting those who are hurting,
or do you find greater joy serving wherever your abilities can meet a need?
Maybe you have a desire to help children know God.
Or perhaps your heart is to serve others with your cooking.
I know women who have turned their passion for crafting, scrapbooking,
and even golfing into ways of reaching out and touching the lives of others.

God's ultimate desire is for you to live passionately for Him—
to care enough about what
He cares about to want to make a difference.
He has given you natural talents, abilities, and spiritual gifts,
so that when they are combined with your unique passions
you become His hands, His heart, and His voice to those around you.

Because I met Jesus and discovered the Truth
that sets people free written upon the pages of my Bible,
I became passionate about it.
I not only had an unquenchable desire to read and study it,
but I also had a desire to share the Word with others.
After many years of God healing and refining my life,
He united my passion with my natural
God~given talents and abilities.
I never cease to thank Him for the wonderfully unique ways
He has given me to personally express His heart
to the world through my art and writing.

It saddens me to say, my passion has not always burned intensely.
There have been times when the flame has been dimmed by the cares of this world, fears,
doubts, and the struggles of life. But as I write this, I am encouraged—and I hope
you will be, too—by the Apostle Paul's reminder to a young man named Timothy.
He told him to stir up or rekindle the flames of the gift God had given him. He was talking
about the gift of the Holy Spirit that gives fuel to our passion and sets our hearts on fire!

Dear God,

Rekindle my faith and stir up any smoldering embers
of my heart so that I may be fully on fire for You.
Unite my passions and my talents in such a unique
and wonderful way that I might bring
great glory to You and incredible blessing to others.

Love God,
your God,
with your
whole heart:
love Him
with all
that's in you,
love Him
with all
you've got!

Deuteronomy 6:5 MSG

PASSION

It's in Christ that we find out
who we are
and what we are living for.

Long before we first heard of Christ
and got our hopes up,
He had His eye on us,
had designs on us for glorious living,
part of the overall purpose
He is working out
in everything and everyone.

Ephesians 1:11, 12 MSG

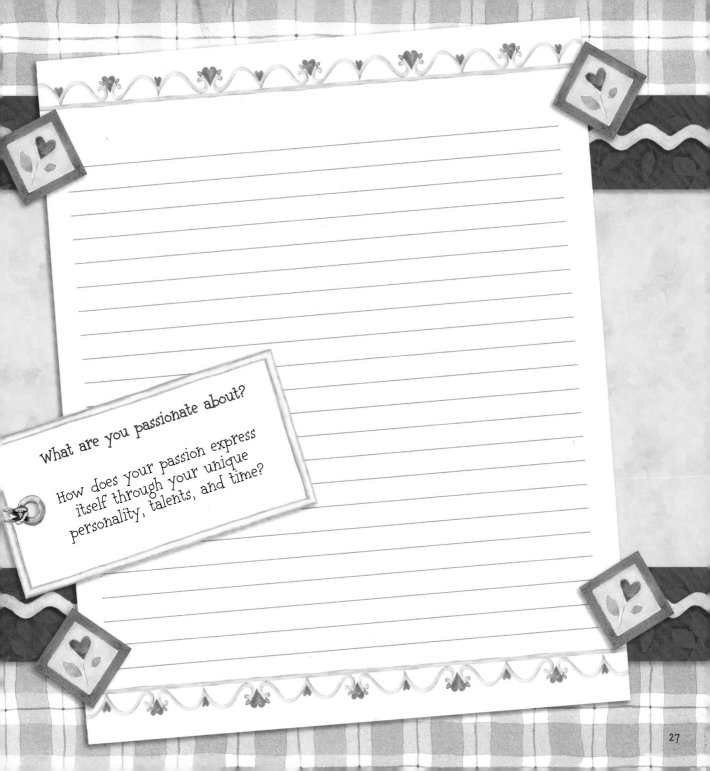

What are you passionate about?

How does your passion express itself through your unique personality, talents, and time?

One
of a
Kind

Personality

A variety of personalities grow in God's garden.
Each one is beautiful to the Lord . . . weaknesses, wormholes, and all!
Even though you probably will see a little of each of these posies in your personality,
I wonder which one you will identify with the most.

The **Popular Petunia** is sincere, fun~loving, and friendly. She laughs a lot and encourages others to laugh along with her. Her not~so~fun side tends to be easily distracted, a bit disorganized, and she can hardly stand to be alone . . . but we gotta love her!

The **Powerful Poppy** is a go~getter. She enjoys being the leader and is good with people and planning. Her leadership qualities can get her into trouble, though. She can be strong~willed and bossy if not kept in check . . . but we can't live without her!

The **Perfect Periwinkle** is a dreamer. She is idealistic and inclines to be both creative as well as detail oriented. Her weak spots are perfectionism, depression, and feelings that are easily hurt . . . but she's definitely a keeper!

The **Peaceful Primrose** is the quiet one. She is easy~going, patient, level~headed, and a pleasure to be with. Her laidback attitude, though, can slip her into an indecisive, unmotivated mode if she's not careful . . . but she's such a blessing!

What a beautiful bouquet of blossoms!

How great God is to create such a variety of colorful characters to fill the earth with the fragrance of His love!

Some flowers can fill a room with the fragrance of spring,
and others fill a heart with joy simply given as a gift.
Some flowers take center stage,
while others are used as fillers in bouquets.
Many flowers have medicinal value,
while others are valued as colorful dyes.

How surprised I was to discover that my husband's mother, my dear friend and mentor mom, was being treated medicinally with a flower! To thin her blood and keep it flowing, she was taking a daily dose of a drug called digitalis that's derived from the lowly foxglove—a flower many of us would classify as a weed! Without it she would have died. Imagine . . . even a lowly flower—in the hands of a pharmacologist, the one who knows its potential—has the incredible power to impact a life for good.

A flower's inherent value is determined by its Creator,
but its worth is not realized until it is used
according to how it was designed.

The same is true of our flowery personalities.
No personality is better than another . . . only different.
God created you with your unique personality,
and because of your particular roots, stem, leaves, and blossoms . . .
you have value like no other!
You cannot be a foxglove if you're a fuchsia,
and you will never be a rhododendron if God made you a rose.
So don't try to be what you're not; rejoice in the flower you are!

The more colorful and thankful you are for who God designed you to be,
the more prolific and fragrant your flowers will grow.

Dear God, show my friend her perfect place
in the floral arrangement of life.
May her blossoms be a fragrant blessing to Your heart.

And remember . . .
every personality, in the hands of the One who knows its potential,
has the power to impact the lives of others for good.

Godliness with contentment is great gain.

1 Timothy 6:6 NKJV

Embrace
what makes you
unique!

What personality types do you identify with most?
In what ways does your personality reflect the character of God?

Do you find yourself complaining about your shape?
Not just your body shape, but the shape of your nose or cheeks or ears?
Do you grumble about the shape of your gifts, talents, or abilities?
Do you ever question God's fairness in how He formed who you are?

There is a passage in the Bible that says,

"Shall what is formed say to Him who formed it,
'Why did you make me like this?'
Does not the potter have the right to make out of the lump of clay
some pottery for noble purposes and some for common use?"

Romans 9:20,21 NIV

You are the Lord's vessel,
fashioned by His hand and for His purposes.

He knows you better than you know yourself,
and He desires only your best.

Some dishes are created for fine dining and others for everyday use.
Some are shaped to serve drinks, while others are made to serve dessert.
Whatever the dish . . .
its shape, size, color, or condition . . .
it is not the serving dish but what is being served that matters most.

God formed you to be a vessel of honor—
one that He can fill up with Himself and pour out on the world.

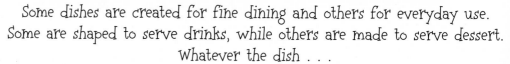

Uniquely His

Your vessel –
God's handiwork

Be encouraged—every day is a new day!
God not only formed you
in your mother's womb, but
He continues to mold and shape you
with each circumstance and struggle.
With every new opportunity
to walk in faith or do what is right,
God is at work in you and through you
shaping your life to best reflect
the glory of His Son.

With every turn of the wheel . . .
God is forming your character to look
more and more like His Son, Jesus.

Sometimes, though,
you may find yourself fighting the Potter,
wanting your own way instead of His.
Dear friend, let Him have His way.
His way is always better than yours!

I have been acutely aware of my own uniqueness most of my life—sometimes painfully so. I was a rather shy, quiet child, so I never fit in with the popular crowd. I was okay smart, but not enough to fit in with the intellectual crowd. I couldn't throw, hit, or catch a ball, so I definitely wasn't included with the athletic crowd. My mother didn't know what to do with me, and no one else did either. Now, I don't tell you this to feel sorry for me; I tell you this so that for a moment you might imagine how I felt when, as a new Christian, I came across a verse in the Bible that says we are a holy nation, a chosen priesthood . . .

a PECULIAR people!

Wonderfully Peculiar

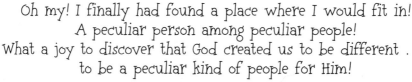

Oh my! I finally had found a place where I would fit in!
A peculiar person among peculiar people!
What a joy to discover that God created us to be different . . .
to be a peculiar kind of people for Him!

It wasn't long until I came to understand
that in more modern translations of
1 Peter 2:9, the word "peculiar" is
rendered "special" because we
are God's SPECIAL people . . .
His pride and joy.

But truth be known, we are all still
a bit peculiar, aren't we?
There is something a little different
about each of us that sets us apart.
The reality is that no matter
how different we are,
we all want and need to fit in . . .
to be loved and accepted
and valued for who we are.

Wonderfully Special

Sometimes the problem is
we don't really know who we are.
We spend all of our lives
trying to be like other people
instead of seeking to be
who God uniquely designed us to be.
Seek and you will find!

I'm a little teapot, short and stout,
Here is my handle, here is my spout.
When I get all steamed up, you'll hear me shout—
"Just tip me over and pour me out!"

You're God's little teapot by design,
Filled with the love of Christ divine.
Let Him mold and shape you, one of a kind—
and pour through you time after time.

What part of your shape do you most struggle with accepting?
Write an "I surrender" prayer to God, putting that particular
lump of your clay back into the Potter's skilled hands
for Him to mold and shape for His glory!

Our natural skills and talents help define who we are. We've all been given particular abilities in order to show who God is—in us and through us.

The Bible says,
"God has given each of us the ability to do certain things well" (Romans 12:6 NLT).
It does not say "all things well" but "certain things well."
So it is a good thing for us to discover, accept, and use our certain talents and abilities that He's given us to serve Him and bless others.
To covet someone else's talent is not only a waste of our precious time but an insult to God, implying that He must have made a mistake in the gifts He's given us.

If you are a saxophone wanting to be a flute, you will never be happy. If you're a drum dreaming of being a cymbal, you'll never dance to the rhythm of your own heart!

But if you will discover the sound of your calling and create your own special music with all your heart, then you will be a joyful noise to the Lord.
And as we all offer up our lives together—as instruments for God's glory, each one playing the harmony we've been given— we become blessings to the heart of God and a

Symphony of Celebration!

MAKE A JOYFUL noise UNTO THE LORD

Psalm 100:1 KJV

...Be thankfu

an

Every day
I will bless You,

And I will
praise Your name
forever and ever.
Psalm 145:2 NKJV

unto Him

bless His name.

Psalm 100:4 KJV

Every good
and perfect gift
is from above.

James 1:17 NIV

Who you are cannot be separated from the talents and abilities
that were woven into the very fiber of your being.
Some people are just naturally good at numbers,
while others love gardening or cooking.
Still others have a natural talent in music or art or mechanics.

Whatever talents and abilities you've been given, they are gifts from
your heavenly Father, and they're not to be taken for granted.
Sometimes you may feel inadequate because your gifts seem so insignificant
compared to others', but the truth is—all talents come from God and have
both earthly and eternal value when used for God's glory.

The sad thing is that when we compare our gifts to another's,
we can end up feeling like we have nothing to offer.
The Bible says to "not withhold good from those who deserve it,
when it is in your power to act" (Proverbs 3:27 NIV).
What abilities do you have that give you the "power to act"?

Can you cook a meal for the homeless or whip up cookies for the bake sale?
Can you hold babies in the nursery or hold prayer meetings in your home?
Can you teach God's Word to children
or teach young women how to care for their families better?

 As you seek to become all God designed you to be,
acknowledge your talents and abilities as His gifts to you,
and look for His opportunities to use them.

Cooking is not my gift—never has been. Oh, I can cook, but many a friend and family member has been entertained by watching my meager attempts in action.

Periodically I get a call from my church asking if I can prepare and deliver a meal to someone in need, and my personality's instinct is always to say "yes." I would lay aside my painting or writing and instead struggle to create with food. One day I had to accept the fact that cooking is simply not my gift, and whenever I said "yes," I actually was depriving others of using their talents to serve the body of Christ in their God-designed ways. I also came to understand that if someone who has the gift to cook chooses not to use it as a blessing to others, then someone else must lay aside her own gifts to serve in a way she's not designed.

Nowadays, I kindly respond to requests about cooking meals by asking callers to put my name at the bottom of the list. I tell them that if they don't have enough cooks by the time they get to my name again, then please call me back because it is still my nature, and Christ's, to meet the need.

This same picture is true for all of us
no matter what our gifts and talents are.
By trying to do it all ourselves, without even realizing it
we might be depriving others of the opportunities to use their gifts.
Let's be careful to do those things that God
has **UNIQUELY GIFTED** us to do so that others can do theirs!

Do not neglect
your gift,
which was given
to you . . .

1 Timothy 4:4: NIV

to~
from~

Get
Well

Just as each of us has one body with many members, and these members do not all have the same function, so in Christ we who are many form one body, and each member belongs to all the others. We have different gifts, according to the grace given us.
If a man's gift is prophesying, let him use it in proportion to his faith.
If it is serving, let him serve;
if it is teaching, let him teach;
if it is encouragement, let him encourage;
if it is contributing to the needs of others, let him give generously to the needs of others;
if it is leadership, let him govern diligently;
if it is showing mercy, let him do it cheerfully.

Romans 12:4, 8 NIV

What are some of the talents, gifts, and abilities God has given you?

Write a prayer, song, or poem of thanksgiving to God as the Giver of these gifts.

To every-
thing
there
is a
season.

Ecclesiastes 3:1

FRUITFUL

Living

I especially love this season of my being!
Life isn't perfect~it won't be this side of heaven~
but I finally am learning to embrace my own uniqueness,
accept the season and circumstances of my life,
and delight in the fruit God is bearing in me and through me.

Like any other fruit tree or vine~in fact, just like you~
I continue to battle cloudy days and stormy weather.
Some of my fruit still has wormholes and bug bites,
but knowing that I am what I am
and you are what you are~totally by the grace of God~
has set me free to be who the Lord created me to be.
I no longer have to try to be like you
or want you to be like me. We're all free to bear fruit
and bless the Lord the way He designed us to.

Jesus said:

"I am the vine, you are the branches.
He who abides in Me, and I in him, bears much fruit;
For without Me you can do nothing."

John 15:5 NKJV

Whatever season you're in—celebrate it!
young or old; married or single;
children, no children, or empty-nester;
prosperous or pauper;
career woman, stay-at-home mom, or both—
you were created for such a time—and season—as this!

Keeping your heart connected to His
is the secret to fruitfulness in every season!

If a peach tree is unruly in the winter
and refuses to be pruned,
it will neither blossom nor bear fruit,
and its life is wasted.

If a peach tree blossoms in the spring,
but frost bites and it never bears fruit,
its beauty is lost in its barrenness.

If a peach tree blossoms in the spring
and bears a bountiful crop of fruit,
but that fruit falls to the ground and rots~
never shared with another~
the tree's purpose is unfulfilled.

But if a peach tree blossoms in the spring
and bears its fruit in due season,
and the sweetness of its flavor
nourishes the life of another,
it rests satisfied
having fulfilled its destiny . . .

Fruitful Living

not to bear apples but peaches~
not for its own glory but for God's~
not for itself but for others.
Now that's fruitful living!

The words we speak are filtered through our own individual personalities, experiences, and emotions, and yet, whether or not we consider ourselves articulate, God wants to use our words to communicate His heart to the world around us.

Fruitful Words

I write books and speak to groups of women, but you also have unique opportunities to share with others. You can use your words to encourage the woman next door who is new to the neighborhood and needs a friend. You can write a note of comfort to the person in your church who needs a daily dose of hope for his or her circumstances. Sometimes you alone are the love of Jesus that someone needs to hear.

If you are a quiet type, you might speak fewer words than someone who is outgoing, but that doesn't mean your words are less important or have less potential to influence the lives of those who hear them. The fruitfulness of your words is determined by the attitude of your heart, not by how many words you speak or how smart you sound.

A few years before I painted my first watercolor,
when I thought I had so little to offer as a blessing to others,
I volunteered to come in early before Bible class
to make the coffee and set up the snack table.
As part of my particular personality, I felt compelled
to bring flowers and other decorations from home
just to dress up the table and make it pretty.

Due to some emotionally painful experiences,
I was in a very withdrawn season of life, and I honestly
could not say more than a few words in a group of women.
I was delighted to be able to come in before everyone else arrived,
set up, and then stay to clean up after everyone else left.
I was not seeking recognition or reward,
but simply to be FRUITFUL — to bless God
and this group of women in some small way.

That choice to step out of my comfort zone
and serve God through serving others,
even in such a small behind-the-scenes way,
definitely was made with fear and trembling.
But because of that one little act of obedience,
doors began to open that I never could have opened myself
even if I had wanted to at that time.

Do not despise this small beginning,
for the eyes of the Lord rejoice
to see the work begin.
Zechariah 4:10 NLT

Every opportunity I was given to serve
required a step of faith that God would enable me
to fulfill that which He was calling me to do.

No one who knew me during that season of my life
ever would have imagined then
that I would be who I am today—
that inside that shy, quiet, hurting woman
was a BUNCH OF FRUIT just waiting
to be born.

At the time, I was working a nine-to-five job
and had never painted a picture in my life.
No one, including me, had a clue that I would be
writing and illustrating books like the one you're
reading today. No one would have imagined that
I would go from being unable to talk in front of even
just a handful of women to being able
to boldly proclaim the love of the Lord to hundreds.
No one had any idea how God would use that
seemingly insignificant act of obedience to fix coffee
—no one, that is, except God.

The Bible tells us not to despise small beginnings . . .
or seasons of change.

You never know where that small act of obedience,
coupled with faith in God, will lead you
or what fruit will be produced!

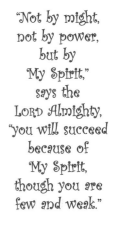

"Not by might,
not by power,
but by
My Spirit,"
says the
LORD Almighty,
"you will succeed
because of
My Spirit,
though you are
few and weak."

Zechariah 4:6 TLB

The fruit of the Spirit

Love

Joy

Peace

Patience

Kindness

Goodness

Faithfulness

Gentleness

Self-Control

Galatians 5:22 NIV

58

What season of life are you in?
Are you accepting this season as part of God's plan and bearing fruit?
If so, write a note of gratitude for the blessings of this time.
If not, ask God to help you blossom and bear much fruit
whatever your season and look forward to what He has in store!

If God gives such attention
to the appearance of wildflowers
—most of which are never even seen—
don't you think he'll attend to you,
take pride in you, do his best for you?

Matthew 6:30 MSG

Style

Man looks at the outward appearance but God looks at the heart.

1 Samuel 16:7 NIV

Just the other day a woman at church
stopped to comment on my new hairdo.
"Stylin'," she said.
"Hmmmm . . ." I thought. "Stylin'—I like that."
But what exactly does that mean?
It sounded sassy . . . and classy . . .
and for a woman my age, that's quite a feat.
I think I'll keep the 'do!

Style is something we all have. We are all stylish in our
own unique ways because style is simply an
outward expression of our inward personalities.

If you are outdoorsy or athletic, most likely you will
dress differently than a bookworm or a romantic.
You might be a woman who loves ruffles and lace,
or you may lean toward the classic and chic.
Jeans may be your pants of choice
or maybe you've never even owned a pair.

The colors and clothes you wear are, in some ways,
reflections of who you are . . . how you view
yourself and want others to view you, as well as
your age, likes and dislikes, and your season of life.

But the style that's most important is your lifestyle!
How you live and the choices you make
are the truest reflections of who you are.
It is your lifestyle that reveals
who you are in Christ and who He is in you!
Are you stylin'?

God created you to be uniquely you, and His desire is to see you be confident in who you are in order for you to fulfill your God~given destiny. But you also have an enemy who seeks to steal away your confidence and keep you from experiencing God's best intentions and purposes for your life.

The devil is not only God's enemy but, because you belong to the Lord, he is your foe, too. His strategy is to keep you down by messing with your mind. It's as if he sits on your shoulder and whispers in your ear, filling your thoughts with lies, doubts, insecurities, and fears, trying his best to keep you focused on your problems instead of the truth and promises of God.

What we think about steers the course of our life much like the rudder of a ship, and the devil knows it. Your attitude—toward yourself, your family and friends, where you live and work, the car you drive, and the challenges of daily life—all starts with what you're thinking.

That's why it is so important for us to read the Bible for ourselves—so we can know God's truth about who we are and align our thoughts with His!

By choosing to let "God thoughts" steer your life and attitude towards yourself, others, and everyday life, your struggles will be transformed. You will have the faith and freedom to fulfill your destiny with confidence.

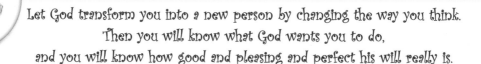

Let God transform you into a new person by changing the way you think.
Then you will know what God wants you to do,
and you will know how good and pleasing and perfect his will really is.

Romans 12:2 NLT

Your attitude
should be the same
as that of
Christ Jesus.
Philippians 2:5 NIV

ATTiTude

63

In our culture we carry our money in a purse ready to spend it wherever we go.

Think of yourself as a purse full of riches, and everywhere you go God wants you to spend the treasures of who you are to bless and encourage the poor in spirit. Do it with style!

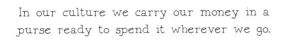

put on joy...

Our hearts ache, but we always have joy.
We are poor,
but we give spiritual riches to others.
We own nothing,
And yet we have everything.

2 Corinthians 6:10 NLT

FAITH

Just as styles change from year to year, so do we. You are not the same person you were five years ago, and neither am I. Not only do we change outwardly as we age, but also as believers in Christ. God is at work in us transforming our lives inwardly from glory to glory.

Sometimes the transition from one glory to the next can be extremely painful. I know this from personal experience. It may require allowing God to do some major surgery to remove something in our lives that hinders us, such as unforgiveness or unbelief, or He might have to open up an old wound and clean it out in order for it to heal properly.

If you're ready to move to the next glory with God, it will require a surrender to His scalpel and a stepping out in faith. You must believe that God is who He says He is, that He can do what He says He can do, that you are who He says you are, and that He will enable and empower you to do whatever He calls you to do.

Getting to your next glory may bring some trials and testing, but believe God . . . it's worth it!

Step Out in Faith

My daughter and I are so much alike in so many ways.
We are both women, wives, moms, and artists.
We live in the same town, go to the same church,
and love just being together.
But we are very different in style.
We dress differently, decorate differently,
and create differently.

Michelle paints with acrylics—I do watercolors.
She uses bright colors—I'm more subdued.
She's whimsical and abstract—I'm more traditional.
She primarily paints designs for her own line of clocks,
while I paint primarily to illustrate God's Word.
Neither one is better—only different.

We have come to accept and even laugh at how most people
tend to love one of our styles but not the other.

We are so much alike . . . and yet so different!
Isn't that the way it is with all of us?

Our differences make us
uniquely usable to God
and are very important
in His plans to bring people to Himself.
Michelle, because of her uniqueness,
can go places and connect with people
who I never could and vice versa.

God wants us to love one another—
not only to delight in our similarities,
but also to embrace our differences.
Remember . . . God can use you in ways
that I would never be qualified,
simply because you are you
and I am not!

Oil of the Spirit

Above all else, put on

LOVE

Colossians 3:14

My darling daughter,

I just wanted to remind you how much I love and adore you. I know I've written you before, many times through many hands, and I so long for you to know how much you mean to me and how much I delight in you.

When you were born I was the proudest Father ever, and I have been every day since. I know you sometimes think you're a disappointment to Me, but you're not . . . nothing you can do or say or think surprises Me or can cause Me to love you any less. Everyone makes mistakes—no one is perfect—but you have no idea how it blesses My heart when you come to Me just as you are.

I was so excited the day you gave your heart to Me. In fact, at the moment that you were born again into heaven's family, all the angels joined Me in singing "Happy Birthday" to you! It was glorious! And I love that we are now one in My Son because I have so many places for us to go and so many people I want us to see together. Don't worry . . . I won't overwhelm you or give you more than you can handle, although I may stretch you a bit to where you will have to depend on Me even more.

Did you know I am enthralled by your beauty? I am. You truly are one of a kind by My design, and I don't make mistakes. I know that sometimes it's hard for you to believe what I say about you is true, but it is—every word of it! What a blessing it would be to Me for you to reread My earlier letters to you.

I am so glad you desire to become all that I have designed you to be. I promise you'll be blessed for it!

With all My love . . . in My Son's Name and for Our glory,
Your heavenly Father

68

Pause a moment to reflect and respond to God's love letter to you on the previous page.

Just imagine if you were a pretty little teacup full of dirt
just sitting outside minding your own business.
You would be a target for every floating seed around,
and soon you would become overgrown with the weeds of the world~
unbelief, pride, unforgiveness, and jealousy,
just to name a few. Hmmm . . . not a pretty sight.

But God created you to be that pretty cup,
your shape, color, purpose, and personality all perfectly delightful.
However, because of the nature of the earthly dirt, weedy seeds
were hidden in the soil of your heart from the day you were created.
And the influences of your life added a few more along the way.
You were helpless and didn't know what to do
so the weeds took root and grew.

But there is such good and glorious news!
As that pretty little teacup
you keep the same unique shape, color, purpose, and personality,
but when you admit that you are helpless and
ask Jesus to be your Savior
you become His and He gives you a new heart!
He dumps out the old dirt and fills you up with good clean soil!
And in place of weeds, you now bloom with the beauty of God's love.

You're a new creation in Christ.
Old things are gone, and all things have been made new!

So why do we still see weeds?
Because as long as we live in this world, weed seeds will sneak into our hearts.
But always REMEMBER what God has done for you!
You are no longer helpless~
you have everything you need in Christ to fight against the weeds and win.

God's Word is the spiritual weed killer of choice!
Pick it up and use it against those pesky sin~weeds
and your blooms will show His glory.

Just to remember God
is a blessing—
now and tomorrow
and always.

Psalm 113:2 MSG

Pansies

Kingdom Seeds
of
Remembrance

71

"I know
the plans
I have for you,"
declares the
LORD,

"plans to
prosper you
and not
to harm you,

plans to
give you hope
and
a future."

Jeremiah 29:11 NIV

72

For most of my life I lived in the country and loved it. When we moved to the city because of my husband's work, I had a hard time. We'd moved several times before, so I just kept waiting for my husband to come home from work and say we were moving again. I was ready. For six years I refused to settle in.

We bought a house but I didn't paint a wall. I went to church but never got involved or got to know anyone. I simply worked my job, took care of our daily needs, and waited for better days. Then one day I heard a voice in my heart—so real it was almost audible—and it was God. He told me I was rebelling, and I protested, "No, Lord, I just don't want to live here." He said, "I know, and that's rebellion." He told me that He had a plan for my life and a purpose for my being there, but as long as I fought against Him I would never see the plan fulfilled or the blessings of it in my life. I asked God to forgive me for my attitude and began seriously thanking Him for my circumstances. With that decision, God turned the page and began writing me a new chapter.

My circumstances didn't change—we didn't move or buy a different house—but my heart was moved and I became a different person.

It is possible to bloom where you're planted when your heart and hope are rooted in the soil of God's incredible love!

God has designed plans and purposes uniquely for you. You are only able to fulfill them as you acknowledge and accept who you are and where you've been planted as part of His sovereign plan for your life.

Savor some moments with the Lord. Ask Him to examine your heart and show you anything that's hindering God's work in your life.

Surrender any areas where you've been fighting God, ask His forgiveness, and begin today to give Him thanks! You won't regret it!

Savored Moments

Be still
and know
that I am
God.
Psalm 46:10

75

My cup
runneth
over.

Psalm 23:15 KJV

Dear Friend,

Thank you for allowing me to share my heart with you through stories and art. This book was more challenging for me than any book before, but I believe the difficulty came because this message has so much potential to touch and change lives. I can only pray and believe that it has been worth the struggle and that it has been like a refreshing drink of God's Spirit to your soul.

Through the pages of this little book, I hope you have discovered some truth . . . not about how great we are, but about how great is the Christ who lives in us and through us . . . and how great is the God who created you and me to be uniquely His and uniquely one of a kind by His design. Because it is only through knowing Him that we can even begin to know ourselves.

How liberating it is to understand that the more we are able to see ourselves through His eyes and not just our own—to see and accept ourselves as God's unique workmanship—the more we are able to love and accept one another and to do the good works He has designed us to do . . . to be His hands, His heart, and His voice to the people around us. And oh, how the world needs us. And oh, how we need each other!

May the Lord wrap His arms around you and love on you like only He can!

In Christ's love and for His glory,
Karla

If you hold to my
teaching, you are really
my disciples. Then you
will know the truth,
and the truth
will set you free.

If the Son sets you free,
you will be free indeed.

Jesus

John 8:31, 32, 36 NIV

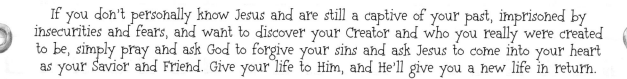

If you don't personally know Jesus and are still a captive of your past, imprisoned by
insecurities and fears, and want to discover your Creator and who you really were created
to be, simply pray and ask God to forgive your sins and ask Jesus to come into your heart
as your Savior and Friend. Give your life to Him, and He'll give you a new life in return.

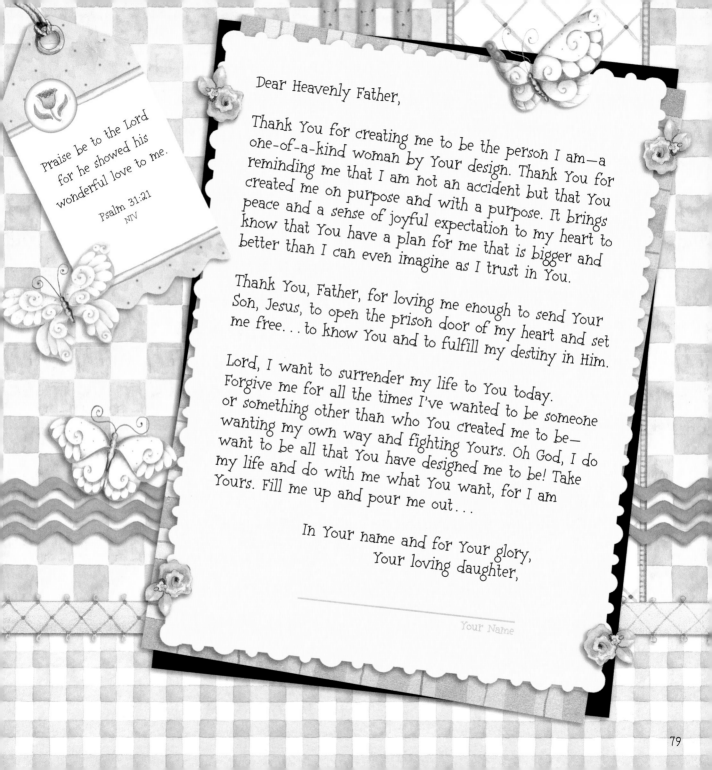

Praise be to the Lord
for he showed his
wonderful love to me.

Psalm 31:21
NIV

Dear Heavenly Father,

Thank You for creating me to be the person I am—a one-of-a-kind woman by Your design. Thank You for reminding me that I am not an accident but that You created me on purpose and with a purpose. It brings peace and a sense of joyful expectation to my heart to know that You have a plan for me that is bigger and better than I can even imagine as I trust in You.

Thank You, Father, for loving me enough to send Your Son, Jesus, to open the prison door of my heart and set me free. . .to know You and to fulfill my destiny in Him.

Lord, I want to surrender my life to You today. Forgive me for all the times I've wanted to be someone or something other than who You created me to be— wanting my own way and fighting Yours. Oh God, I do want to be all that You have designed me to be! Take my life and do with me what You want, for I am Yours. Fill me up and pour me out. . .

In Your name and for Your glory,
Your loving daughter,

_____
Your Name